**History Beneath Your Feet**

**Titles in this series**

Ancient Egypt
Ancient Greece

KT-382-965

Editor: Jonathan Ingoldby
Series design: Christopher Halls at Mind's Eye Design
Illustrations and project artwork: John Yates
Production controller: Carol Stevens
Consultant: Dr Philip deSouza, St Mary's College,
University of Surrey

First published in Great Britain in 1999 by
Wayland (Publishers) Ltd,
Reprinted in 2000 by Hodder Wayland,
an imprint of Hodder Children's Books
This paperback edition published in 2003

© Hodder Wayland 1999

Hodder Children's Books
A division of Hodder Headline Limited
338 Euston Road, London NW1 3BH

**British Library Cataloguing in Publication Data**
Hicks, Peter, 1952-
   Ancient Greece. - (History beneath your feet)
   1.Greece - Antiquities - Juvenile literature 2.Greece -
   History - Juvenile literature
   I.Title
   938

ISBN 0-7502-4448-8

Printed and bound in Italy by G. Canale & C.Sp.A.,
Turin

Cover photographs: The Tholos at Delphi (Michael
Holford); 'Mask of Agamemnon' (AKG)

The publishers would like to thank the following for
permission to publish their pictures

Lesley & Roy Adkins 19, 21, 24, 32; AKG (London) 6, 7,
9, 10, 18, 30, 36, 37; Ancient Art and Architecture
Collection 28; C.M. Dixon 14, 23, 26; Robert Harding
4–5, 16, 38; Peter Hicks 11, 17, 41, 42; Michael Holford
15, 22, 33; Norma Joseph 8, 12–13, 40, 43; Planet Earth
Pictures 34; John Prague, The Manchester Museum,
University of Manchester 31, 35; Wayland Picture
Library 27, 39

**All Hodder Wayland books encourage children to read and help them improve their literacy.**

 The contents page, page numbers, headings and index help locate specific pieces of information.

 The glossary reinforces alphabetic knowledge and extends vocabulary.

 The further information section suggests other books dealing with the same subject.

 Find out more about how this book is specifically relevant to the National Literacy Strategy on page 47.

Tegan

# ANCIENT GREECE

## PETER HICKS

HODDER
*Wayland*

an imprint of Hodder Children's Books

# CONTENTS

## WHAT IS ARCHAEOLOGY?

'Archaeology' is a Greek word meaning 'the study of ancient things'. Archaeologists study the remains of people, buildings and objects from earlier times and then piece together what life had been like in the past. Some of these remains are so old that they have become hidden by earth or more recent buildings. This means that archaeologists first have to find where these remains are hidden, and then dig down or 'excavate' to see what is there. This is why so much history is 'beneath your feet'.

# WHO WERE THE ANCIENT GREEKS?

Greece is a beautiful, mountainous country surrounded and indented by the sea. Only about 20 per cent of the land is suitable for growing crops, making agriculture very difficult. Even the Mediterranean Sea – essential for food and transport – contains strong currents and winds that test the best sailors.

MACEDONIA

Pella

Vergina • • Olynthus

• Troy

AEGEAN SEA

ASIA MINOR

Delphi •

Corinth • • Athens

Olympia • • Mycenae

Pylos •

IONIAN SEA

PELOPONNESE

Knossos •

CRETE

The ancient Greeks lived on the mainland and islands of Greece, and also colonized other parts of the ancient world. The harshness of their country may be why they achieved so much. Through hard work their settlements became prosperous – often in the face of terrible disasters such as earthquakes, famine, plague and war.

The civilization now called Classical Greece began around 650 BC. At this time Greece was not one country but made up of many independent 'city states', each of which was called a *polis*. Despite the fact that the city states were often at war with one another, together they produced exceptional art, architecture, theatre, poetry, music and philosophy, as well as founding the now world-famous Olympic Games.

What we know about the ancient Greeks has had to be 'pieced together' from the evidence that remains: ruins of their buildings, ancient inscriptions and writings and individual artefacts. This is the job of the archaeologist.

*The ruins of the temple of Apollo at Corinth.*

# EARLY CIVILIZATIONS IN GREECE

The first civilization of the Greek world was on the island of Crete. The inhabitants became very wealthy by trading their wheat, olive oil and wine with other parts of the Mediterranean. Around 2000 BC, large, impressive palaces were built at Knossos, Phaistos and Zakros.

*The restored throne room at Knossos with its beautiful wall paintings. Sir Arthur Evans thought the throne belonged to a woman so he called it the 'Throne of Ariadne' (the daughter of King Minos).*

## HOW PALACES AND CITIES ARE 'LOST'

When a palace or city is abandoned – or destroyed, as Knossos was – a number of things may happen.

- It might be 'robbed' of building materials for use in another building.

- Even if this does not happen, over time the roof timbers rot, the roof collapses onto the floor, and the weakened walls fall in on themselves.

- The site may be levelled and a new building placed over the original foundations.

- In the countryside, soil and vegetation will build up or grow over the remains, hiding them completely.

The civilization on Crete lasted for over a thousand years until it was destroyed by two key events. Around 1626 BC the volcanic island of Thera, 90 kilometres north of Crete, erupted, causing flooding and earthquakes which destroyed many buildings. Then, around 1450 BC, fierce warriors from Mycenae on mainland Greece conquered Crete.

An Englishman, Sir Arthur Evans (1851–1941), began excavating the Palace of Knossos in 1900. The palace ruins covered 2.2 hectares and the ground plan suggested the labyrinth associated with the legendary King Minos. As a result, Evans named the civilization of Crete 'Minoan'.

Evans is regarded as one of the first 'scientific' archaeologists to work in Greece. He kept a detailed log book or 'site diary' of his work, and pioneered the use of photography to record the stages of the dig. He built high observation towers so that the whole site could easily be photographed. Up to that time archaeologists had only made sketches of sites, and then only when they came across a major find. The great advantage of photographs is that they provide a quick and accurate record of a site long after finds have been removed to museums or the diggings have been filled in again.

*Sir Arthur Evans, the excavator of Knossos. He is holding a copy of a bull's head found at the bottom of a well.*

# THE MYCENAEANS

The Mycenaeans who invaded Crete came from the southern part of the Greek mainland, known as the Peloponnese. Graves found on the mainland tell us that they were a wealthy civilization based on trade over land and sea. The remains of weapons show that they built up a large army, equipped with bronze plate armour. The poet Homer tells us that it was the king of Mycenae who led the Greeks against the city of Troy in Asia Minor (Turkey) – the legendary Trojan War.

The exact site of the city of Troy remained unidentified until modern times. This was partly because archaeologists thought that the Trojan legend was no more than that, and 'Troy' did not exist at all.

The German archaeologist Heinrich Schliemann proved them wrong. Between 1870 and 1890 he excavated on a large scale at the 'Hisarlik mound' in Turkey, which he believed was the site of the legendary city. Because he thought that Troy must be in the lowest level of the mound, he dug carelessly through the upper levels, destroying a great deal of valuable evidence.

Schliemann was desperate to find the grave of Agamemnon, the Mycenaean commander of the Greek force. At Mycenae in 1876, ignoring all the wishes of the Greek government who wanted a small dig, he smashed his way through the site, destroying important Greek and Roman remains. Discovering five shaft graves inside the acropolis he found enough treasure 'to fill a museum'.

*The shaft graves at Mycenae. The ancient Greek poet Homer's comment that 'Mycenae was rich in gold' was proved correct by Schliemann, who found numerous gold artefacts in the graves.*

# PROJECT: THE GOLD MASK OF 'AGAMEMNON'

**You will need:**
**Modelling clay**
**Gold or yellow paint**
**Varnish**
**Cocktail stick**

1. Make a ball about the size of your fist from the modelling clay.

2. Flatten and shape the ball so that it will cover your face.

3. Make and shape two sausages of clay for the lips. Make and shape another sausage for the nose. Attach these to the mask.

4. Shape two balls of clay for the ears, and two more for the eyes. Attach to the mask.

5. Use the cocktail stick to scratch on the eyebrows, beard and moustache.

6. Paint the mask gold (or yellow). Allow to dry, then varnish.

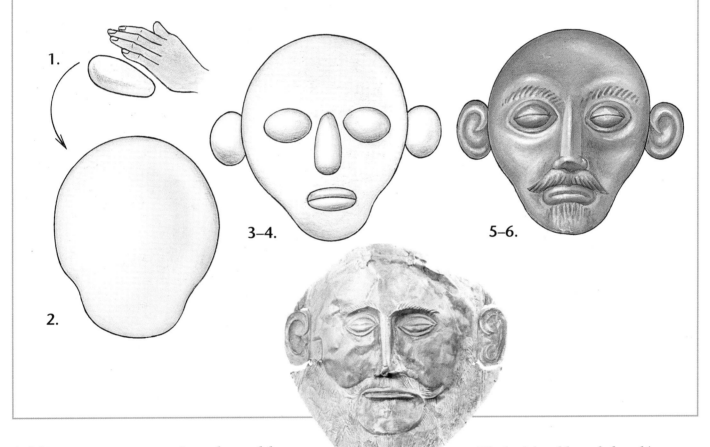

Schliemann was convinced a gold-masked body was Agamemnon. Unfortunately, the mask was 300 years older than the Trojan War (which probably took place around 1250 BC) and there were rumours that Schliemann had 'planted' some of the finds.

*The lavish gold mask found in one of the graves of Mycenae. Schliemann claimed it was the 'face of Agamemnon' but some archaeologists believe he added the moustache to make it more king-like.*

# CLASSICAL GREECE

In time, the Mycenaens grew weaker and tribes invaded Greece from the north. By 1100 BC most Mycenaen towns and palaces had been destroyed or abandoned. Greece entered a period known as the 'dark age', because no written evidence has survived to tell archaeologists and historians about what happened during that time.

The dark age lasted until about 800 BC. By 650 BC Greece had begun to prosper again, and the city states were founded. Temples and public buildings were constructed and cities flourished. The Greeks established colonies in southern Italy, Sicily, western Turkey and parts of north Africa. The age of 'Classical Greece' had begun.

*The agora, or market-place, at Ephesos. Although in Anatolia (modern-day Turkey), Ephesos was regarded as an important city in the Greek homeland.*

## JOHN TURTLE WOOD

In 1860 the British Museum funded the railway engineer John Turtle Wood to search for treasures in Greece. He discovered and 'excavated' the Temple of Artemis at Ephesos. He calculated that he shifted 132,227 cubic feet of 'spoil'. How much important evidence – pottery, metal objects, human remains – was thrown away in the process it is impossible to guess.

The remains of classical Greece have always fascinated Europeans, but during the late nineteenth and early twentieth centuries this fascination turned into a 'craze'. 'Treasure hunters' plundered Greece of its valuable artefacts, sending them to museums in their home countries. There was much rivalry between museums to obtain the 'best' finds. Because the museums funded many of the expeditions, they were able to put pressure on the 'archaeologists' to unearth treasures as quickly as possible. This did not encourage careful excavation.

## FIELD WALKING

Unlike the treasure hunters of the nineteenth century, modern archaeologists are extremely scientific and methodical in their search for the history beneath our feet. A suspected site is often 'field walked' before any digging begins. This involves close inspection of the ground. An area is divided into grid squares, and each walker has to scour the surface of 'their' squares for pottery, brick, tile or glass – in fact, any 'man-made' objects. These may be evidence of a site underground, and where these surface finds run out might mark the boundary of the site.

*After field walking, archaeologists search for structures under the surface. This resistivity meter passes an electric current into the ground. High resistance may suggest a building; low resistance a ditch or pit.*

# THE THEATRE AT EPIDAUROS

Archaeologists are tremendously interested in Classical Greece because it is regarded as the beginning of European civilization. The work and ideas of its mathematicians, philosophers, playwrights, architects, writers and artists have had a huge impact on the Western world.

For example, our modern theatre owes a lot to Classical Greece. The word itself comes from the Greek *theatron*, meaning 'seeing place'. Careful excavation of ancient Greek theatres has led to a greater understanding of how they worked. The best preserved and most famous ancient Greek theatre is at Epidauros in the Peloponnese. It is still used today for performances of Greek tragedies and comedies.

Archaeologists found that the theatre at Epidauros consisted of a huge 'orchestra' – 23 metres in diameter – in which the chorus danced and sang. The actors stood on a raised stage called a *proskension*, 24 metres long by 2.5 metres wide. Behind this, archaeologists discovered the *skene* – the actors' changing room, from which we got our word 'scene'.

The excavations showed that the auditorium (seating area) was built in two phases. The first phase consisted of 34 rows of seats, which held 6,200 spectators. Later another 24 rows were added, increasing the capacity to 12,300. The whole theatre, carved into the side of Mount Konyortos is a breathtaking sight.

*The theatre at Epidauros covers a huge area and the seats are divided into 12 sections. The theatre was badly damaged by the invading Goths in AD 267.*

## RESTORATION TECHNIQUES

Ancient buildings are often badly damaged and need to be restored. When the theatre at Epidauros was excavated it was found that the support walls and seating at the edges had collapsed. Working up from the original foundations and using similar stone, archaeologists were able to rebuild the damaged areas.

# ATHENS

By the middle of the fifth century BC Athens had become the largest and wealthiest city state in the Classical Greek world, and had an impressive army and navy. The city originated from the famous Acropolis, a high, rocky outcrop that was a natural fortress strengthened by huge stone walls. As the city expanded, the central market-place, known as the agora, became an increasingly important civic and religious centre. It was surrounded by government buildings such as council chambers and law courts, and contained two 'stoas': covered market halls to shelter traders and shoppers in hot or wet weather.

## THE AGORA

By the early twentieth century the agora had completely disappeared under the houses of 7,000 modern Athenians. More and more people were coming to live in Athens and in 1924 the Greek government decided to excavate the agora before it was too late. However they did not have enough money to buy out all the inhabitants, knock down their houses and begin digging! Fortunately, in 1927 the American millionaire John D. Rockefeller donated $250,000 to the government, allowing the project to go ahead.

*The agora and stoa of Attalos in Athens, dominated by the Acropolis. The stoa was rebuilt by the Americans in the 1930s and today is a museum housing the finds from the agora.*

The excavation was carried out by the American School of Classical Studies. They demolished 365 buildings and between 1931 and 1939 dug 250,000 tons of 'spoil'. It was a well-organized excavation which showed that much of the agora consisted of shops, workshops and stalls selling items such as pots, bronze and marble statues, lamps, shoes, olive oil, meat and fish.

Evidence of Athenian democracy was also found at the agora. An 'allotment machine' was discovered, which was used to randomly choose jury members for trials. Water clocks were also found, which were used to time the speeches made in court. This meant that the speeches for the defence and those for the prosecution were always the same length, making sure that trials were fair and balanced.

*Excavations being carried out at the agora in Athens.*

## STRATIGRAPHY

An archaeological site like the agora in Athens usually has different layers of 'occupation'. The deeper the layer, the older it is, and any artefact discovered in a lower layer will be older than those nearer the surface. When archaeologists cut a 'section' through a site (which looks a bit like a layer cake with a slice removed), all the strata (layers) can be seen and understood. Pottery, coins and other artefacts found at each level help archaeologists to decide how old that level is.

*An archaeological 'section'. Can you work out the oldest and most recent objects?*

# THE ACROPOLIS

The buildings of the Acropolis have always been of great interest to archaeologists because of what they tell us about ancient Greek life.

The most famous building is the Parthenon, which was completed in 432 BC and is a temple dedicated to Athena, the goddess of wisdom, arts and crafts.

When it was excavated, archaeologists found that the interior of the Parthenon contained a very large inner shrine (called a *cella*), divided into two rooms. Ancient Greek writings told archaeologists that the east room once contained a 12-metre high statue of Athena made from solid gold. They found evidence of this in the form of a rectangular depression in the ground where the statue probably once stood.

*The Acropolis (which means 'high city'), seen from the south-west. It stands on a huge limestone cliff over 153 metres tall, 265 metres long and 153 metres wide.*

The smaller west room originally housed the women who served Athena, although Greek writers tell us that this was later used as the treasury of Athens.

Excavations have uncovered a large number of animal bones: the remains of sacrifices to the goddess. Other items used for worship have also been discovered, such as marble and bronze statues, bowls, marble basins and altars.

*Figures from the left side of the east pediment of the Parthenon. The male figure is thought to be Herakles or Dionysus while the women are the goddesses Demeter, Persephone and Hebe.*

## THE ELGIN MARBLES

Lord Thomas Elgin (1766–1841), a British diplomat and art collector, was sent to Athens to collect works of art and prevent France from dominating this 'trade'. In July 1801 Elgin ordered the seizing of the last remaining statues from the Parthenon and other parts of the Acropolis, as well as 55 marble slabs from a frieze in the Parthenon. Many people, notably the famous poet Lord Byron, were outraged at what they saw as 'vandalism', but Elgin argued that he had permission from the Turkish government. Because the Turks were occupying Greece at that time, the Greek authorities were powerless to stop the 'theft' of their archaeological heritage. In 1816 Elgin sold the marbles to the British Museum, where they can still be seen.

# CITIES AND TOWNS

The Greeks were great city builders, but although many were built in Greece and its colonies, none have survived intact. Many were destroyed by enemies of the Greeks, especially the Romans, and the remains of most of them are hidden beneath other settlements built during the last 2,500 years. However, archaeologists have managed to excavate within modern cities and discover classical remains, and have found abandoned settlements in the countryside whose foundations were hidden by soil and vegetation.

The impressive city of Argos in southern Greece flourished between the seventh and third centuries BC. Careful excavation has revealed the city's agora, with its council chamber, hall, shrine, *odeon* (a small theatre for music and poetry recitals) and theatre.

*The south entrance of the agora at Corinth. There were 33 shops here and from the evidence of the jugs and cups found, most of them sold wine!*

Archaeology has taught us that many Greek colonies throughout the Mediterranean were heavily based on farming. Aerial photographs of the town of Metapontum in southern Italy have revealed numerous field boundaries and farms which surrounded the coastal town. The grain produced by farming communities like this was shipped home to feed the growing Greek population.

*Archaeologists are interested in the small objects found at town sites as well as the buildings. Sieving through the 'spoil' of an excavation is a good way of finding them.*

## AERIAL ARCHAEOLOGY

One of the best ways of locating a site is from the air. Many archaeologists take photographs of the landscape from aeroplanes, and then study the pictures for any tell-tale signs of a site. These may be 'shadow marks' caused by bumps and hollows on the surface which can be seen when the sun is low in the sky. The marks are often traces of buildings or pits beneath the surface. In ploughed fields, aerial photographs can reveal 'soil marks' which are brought to the surface as a result of the ploughing.

Crops too can reveal evidence of sites beneath them: they will ripen faster and be lighter in colour if there is a lack of moisture in the soil caused by hidden walls or foundations. On the other hand, pits or ditches under the ground will hold moisture and the crops above will be greener and grow taller than those surrounding them. These signs are called 'crop marks' and are very easy to spot on an aerial photograph.

Aerial photographs are also used to understand a site once it has been discovered. Old field boundaries, field strips and ancient trackways invisible on the ground appear obvious when see from the air.

# OLYNTHUS AND PELLA

The settlement that tells us most about Greek housing is Olynthus is the Chalcidice region of northern Greece. In 348 BC King Philip of Macedonia accused Olynthus of sheltering his enemies and destroyed the city. The Greek orator Demosthenes said of the disaster: 'Later generations will scarcely believe a city had been on this site'. He was proved wrong: by archaeology.

Olynthus was partly excavated between 1928 and 1934 by an American team of archaeologists from the School of Classical Studies. They found that the inhabitants of Olynthus lived in small square houses with three or four rooms opening onto an internal courtyard. This helped to keep out the noise and dirt from the busy streets. The north side of the courtyard – known as a *loggia* – was covered, and designed to catch the low winter sun. The walls were made with sun-dried mud bricks, which are warm in the winter and cool in the summer. To prevent damp, the walls were built on stone foundations, and then plastered and painted.

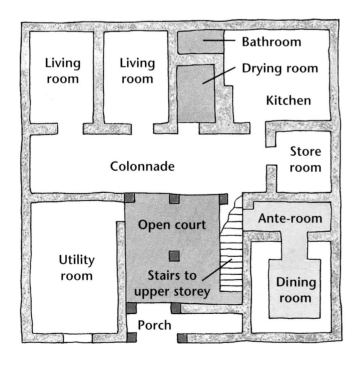

Living room

Living room

Bathroom

Drying room

Kitchen

Store room

Colonnade

Ante-room

Open court

Utility room

Stairs to upper storey

Dining room

Porch

Paving or cement

Mosaic

Wooden column

*A ground plan of a typical ancient Greek house. Excavations have revealed that such houses were built in blocks of ten, surrounded by streets on all sides.*

Many of the floors at Olynthus are decorated with pebble mosaics, and it seems that some houses were very expensive indeed. Archaeologists found a record of the sale of one: 'Dionysion' bought it for 3,500 drachmas – the equivalent of 10 years wages for a skilled workman of the time!

The town of Pella is also in northern Greece, and was also destroyed, this time by the Romans in 168 BC. It was said that so much treasure was plundered from Pella that the triumphal procession in Rome took a whole day! Excavation of Pella revealed an impressive town house known as the 'House of the Lion Hunt' – the subject of a wonderful floor mosaic found there.

*The mosaic floor of 'The House of Dionysus' at Pella.*

# SANCTUARIES AND TEMPLES

Religion was a hugely important part of everyday life in ancient Greece, and the most sacred religious sites were the sanctuaries. Archaeological excavations have revealed that these were often highly complicated sites containing temples, treasuries, bronze and marble statues, theatres, gymnasia and stadia (running tracks).

One of the most sacred sanctuaries was Delphi in central Greece. This was a sanctuary to the god Apollo and also contained the famous 'oracle' which was said to offer advice to people based on the wisdom of Apollo. High above the sanctuary is a stadium where the Pythian games were originally held every eight years. There is also a theatre which was used for musical contests. We know this because inscriptions of hymns to Apollo were discovered, which were so well preserved that they were revived in Greece in the 1930s!

*The Tholos at Delphi. 'Tholos' means 'round building' or 'dome', and this magnificent structure was constructed around 380 BC by the architect Theodorus. Made entirely from marble and surrounded by 20 columns, archaeologists are not sure what it was used for.*

Excavations of Delphi, directed by the French School of Archaeology, began in 1892. The temple sanctuary was a large, roughly rectangular area enclosed by a wall. A sacred way lined with monuments wound up through the sanctuary to the temple of Apollo. The oracle was in a chamber at the rear of the temple.

Other sanctuaries have been found at Olympia (home of the Olympic Games), Epidauros, Corinth and many other places.

## VOTIVE OFFERINGS

People who visited a sanctuary to ask the god's blessing and favour had to offer the god a gift. Gifts were known as 'votive offerings'. People seeking cures for illness at the sanctuary of Corinth offered a terracotta (clay) model of the affected part of the body. Archaeologists have found models of legs, feet, arms, hands, eyes and torsos.

One model, of a left hand, showed a large growth, perhaps a tumour or an abscess, providing evidence of one type of illness the god was asked to cure.

*Votive offerings were an important way of pleasing the gods. Here a group of actors from Athens offer a play to Dionysus in their Spring Festival.*

# EXCAVATING THE SANCTUARIES

E ven using modern methods the sanctuaries are not easy sites to excavate. Delphi, for example, is on different levels on the side of a steep hill, and each level has several 'layers', each of which has to be carefully examined before moving on to the next.

Despite careful cataloguing and measurement of artefacts and buildings, some modern archaeologists feel that we still do not really understand how a sanctuary worked. This may be because useful clues in the form of archaeological evidence were lost or overlooked during previous excavations.

*Excavations at the shrine of Pelops, Olympia. Pelops won a chariot race at Olympia by removing the pins from the wheels of his rival charioteers!*

# PROJECT: MAKE YOUR OWN DELPHIC TEMPLE

**You will need:**
12 cardboard tubes from kitchen rolls
6 small toothpaste boxes
Cardboard from cereal packets
Gummed paper tape
1 large flat side from a cardboard box, approx. 45 x 50 cms square
Paints
Paint brushes

1. Construct a four-sided box 17 x 28 x 22 cms and cut out a doorway at each of the narrow ends. Use the gummed paper tape to stick the box to the base. This is the 'inner *cella*'. Paint on a stonework effect.

2. Stick the 12 cardboard tubes around the *cella* to represent columns: four at each narrow end and two at each side. Paint the columns with bright colours.

3. Paint the toothpaste boxes and stick them along the tops of the columns. These form the base of the roof.

4. Cut out an appropriately-sized piece of cardboard for the roof. Fold it down the middle and place it over the columns.

5. Check the angles at both ends of the temple and cut out two triangles for the pediments. Draw figures, colour them in and stick them to the pediments. Paint the roof red.

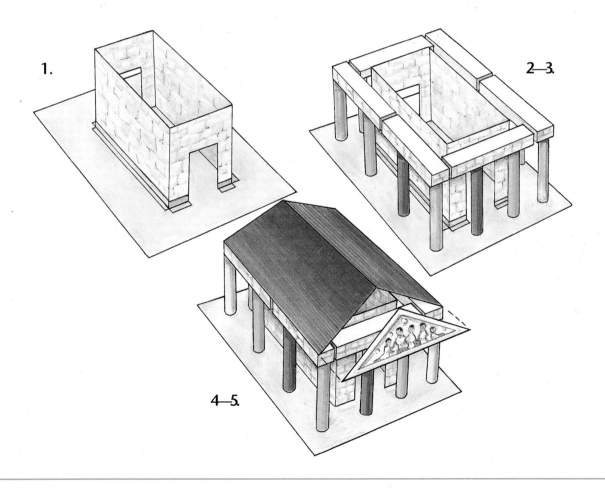

# WARFARE

Greek military strength was based on two important things: the hoplite army made up of closed ranks of well-protected foot soldiers, and naval strength from the lethal war galleys called triremes.

## HOPLITES

Our knowledge of hoplite armour comes from archaeology. Warrior graves have been discovered all over Greece, as well as marble carvings and paintings of soldiers on pottery. The most important piece of equipment was the shield, because it allowed the soldier to cover a large part of his own body and some of the body of the comrade on his left when in tight formation. Shields were about 80 centimetres in diameter and were faced and rimmed with bronze. The rest of the shield was probably made of wood or leather: only the bronze survives because wood and leather perish and disintegrate over time.

A hoplite's head was protected by a helmet beaten from a single sheet of bronze. Other equipment included leg-guards, chest and shoulder pieces, a sword and a spear.

*A superb suit of hoplite armour, from an eighth-century BC grave at Argos. The helmet and breastplate are both made of bronze. This is the oldest suit of armour to be found in Greece to date.*

# THE BATTLE OF MARATHON

One of the most famous battles of the Persian Wars (499–478 BC) was the battle of Marathon in 490 BC. Although heavily outnumbered, the Greeks (made up of Athenian and Plataean warriors) managed to defeat the powerful Persian army. The Athenians lost 192 warriors in the fighting, and they were buried under a huge burial mound ('soros'), 10 metres high and 200 metres in circumference. The soros was excavated in 1890 and archaeologists discovered the ashes of cremated warriors, the bones of animal sacrifices and some pottery.

In 1970, the smaller soros of the Plataean dead was discovered. Excavations revealed 11 skeletons of men in their twenties, one 12-year-old boy and one man aged about 40, probably an officer. All this helped archaeologists to understand the burial ceremonies of dead warriors and the type of offerings and sacrifices that were made to the gods at an ancient Greek warrior funeral. Different types of sword, arrow heads and bullet-shaped slingshots provided valuable clues about how the battle was fought.

*Two hoplite warriors fighting. The bronze rail at the centre of a hoplite's shield allowed it to be held even if the hand was doing something else.*

# TRIREMES

Triremes were oar-powered warships famous for their speed, which helped the Greek city states beat the Persians at the battle of Salamis in 480 BC. Evidence such as inscriptions and the writings of Greek authors shows that these ships had 170 oarsmen, which meant that they could reach speeds of up to 13 kilometres per hour. This allowed them to attack enemy ships using a bronze-clad ram which pierced their hulls and sank them.

## THE *OLYMPIAS*: A TRIREME SAILS AGAIN

Historians and engineers recently used all the evidence they had collected about triremes to build one themselves and sail it around the Mediterranean. This helped them to learn more about what triremes were like to sail and row, how fast they could go, how easily they could be turned around quickly and how far they could travel in a day.

*The* Olympias *at full speed. As well as being fighting platforms, the decks of a trireme offered protection for the rowers.*

The oarsmen were arranged on three levels along each side of the ship: 31 on the top level, 27 in the middle and 27 at the bottom. The oars were prevented from colliding with one another by an 'outrigger' for the top level of rowers so that their oars struck the water slightly further out and at a steeper angle. Sails were used for power when the trireme was not in a battle.

# PROJECT: MAKE YOUR OWN TRIREME

**You will need:**
**A piece of card 50 x 40 cms**
**Scissors**
**Paints**
**Scrap paper**
**Drinking straws**

1. Draw one side of your trireme onto the card. It needs to be about 35 cms long. Cut it out and then draw round the shape to make a second, identical side. Use the scissors to punch the oarholes (in sets of three) into the hull. Glue the sides into a simple boat shape.

2. Put a piece of scrap paper over the top of the ship and draw the outline of the deck. Allow an extra 1 cm all the way around the edge.

3. Cut out and paint the deck and the sides of the hull. Make small cuts around the edge of the deck shape, turn up the edge and glue it into the hull.

4. Carefully split the ends of the straws and insert small pieces of card for the paddles. Slide the oars into the oarholes.

5. Cut out a steering oar and stick it to the side of the ship at the stern (rear). Add a pointed ram made from card and cut back the prow (front) to the correct shape. Add a curved piece of card to the stern.

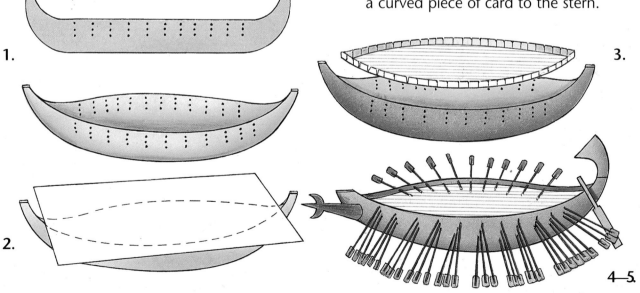

# SCIENCE AND HEALTH

Classical Greece is justly famous for its scientific and medical ideas. Hippocrates (469–399 BC), who is often called the 'father of medicine', pioneered the idea of scientifically observing a patient as a way of understanding disease. His ideas on diet and treatment are still regarded today as being thousands of years ahead of their time.

Archaeologists have found portable medical cases used by ancient Greek doctors when visiting their patients. They contained bronze instruments such as tongs, scalpels, spatulas and spoons, and had tiny compartments for different drugs. Many doctors became very experienced in treating wounds and broken bones by serving in the army, and were often called to the *palaistra* (the gymnasium or wrestling ground) to set broken arms or legs.

*A Greek vase painting showing a doctor bleeding a man's arm. This was done to remove the 'bad blood' or impurities from the patient.*

## THE SECRETS OF SKELETONS

Modern archaeological techniques help us to study and learn about the health of ancient peoples and the environment in which they lived. A skeleton can reveal evidence about the age, sex, diet and general health of the person when they were alive.

The sex of a skeleton is usually identified by the size of the skull and the width of the pelvis. 'Harris lines' – tiny cracks in the bones caused by famine, illness or wounding – show when bone growth began and when it stopped. The position of the lines in relation to the long arm or leg bones tells archaeologists at what age in the person's life such problems occurred.

Skeletons of the ancient Greeks have revealed that many suffered from osteoarthritis – painful stiffness in the joints. This shows up in skeletons as wear and tear in the large weight-bearing joints of the knee, hip and spine.

## FACIAL RECONSTRUCTION

Archaeologists can use the skulls of people found at sites to reconstruct what their faces were like. A cast of the skull is made and then the depth of the muscle tissue worked out from the age and sex of the skeleton. Experts then use modelling clay to 'bring the person to life'. One of the most famous reconstructions is that of King Philip II of Macedonia, destroyer of Olynthus and father of Alexander the Great.

*Richard Neave's incredible reconstruction of the head of Philip II was made from the remains of a skull found in the royal tomb at Vergina, Macedonia. Philip's disfigured eye was probably the result of a sword blow during one of his many battles.*

# TRANSPORT

The development of transport networks in ancient Greece came as a result of the geography. Despite the steep, craggy mountains, the ancient Greeks built roads, although the sheer size of the mountains made this a difficult and expensive task.

On flatter land, roads tended to be dirt tracks, and roadside accommodation was provided for travellers. We know this because a large hostel containing 160 rooms was excavated at the sanctuary of Epidauros. Poor people usually walked from place to place. Richer people probably rode horses. A record of a horse being hired out has survived and was discovered in Athens.

Because Greece is surrounded by water, merchant ships were used for carrying heavy cargoes over long and short distances. Ports were built on all the main islands and around the mainland to load or unload goods being delivered from all over the Mediterranean. Many harbour walls still in use today date back to the Classical Greek era – for example, those on the islands of Samos and Delos.

*The remains of the hostel used by visitors to Epidauros. Nearby was the important bath house where weary and dusty travellers cleaned up after their long journey.*

*A slow, heavy merchant ship with a faster, two-level warship. Note the sharp, bronze ram, used to sink enemy ships.*

Ancient Greek pottery paintings show that merchant ships came in all shapes and sizes, but did have a number of similarities. Most were steered from the stern by one man holding two steering oars. They had rectangular sails attached to the central mast by a yard (beam of wood). By turning the sail using the yard it was possible to sail slightly into the wind, a technique known today as 'tacking'.

## SHORTCUT BY SLIPWAY

An incredible example of ancient Greek technology and engineering was excavated on the isthmus (thin strip of land) between Attica and the Peloponnese that separates the Saronic Gulf from the Gulf of Corinth. Instead of sailing round the long way by sea, the ancient Greeks built a *diolkis*, or slipway, right across the isthmus so that ships could be hauled across on trolleys pulled by oxen. Deep ruts caused by the trolley wheels are still visible in the stone road.

# THE KYRENIA SHIP

Underwater archaeology has helped archaeologists to understand a lot more about ancient Greek merchant ships and their cargoes. One of the most exciting underwater discoveries was the 'Kyrenia Ship', a fourth-century BC merchant ship found 1 kilometre off Kyrenia, in Cyprus. Well-preserved in 30 metres of water, it was excavated in the late 1960s.

The cargo found on board was impressive: 404 amphorae (storage jars) of wine, 10,000 almonds and 29 assorted mill stones, which were probably used as ballast to keep the ship stable in the water. Four sets of clay jugs, cups, spoons and plates indicated a crew of four men. The pottery was traced to the island of Rhodes, so this was probably the ship's home port. A coin found on board was dated to 306 BC, so the last voyage of the Kyrenia Ship must have taken place after this date.

*Divers carefully excavating a section of a wreck in the Mediterranean Sea. The sand and silt on the sea bed often preserve wood and leather objects.*

Archaeologists have pieced together what they think were the ship's 'last moments'. Eight spearheads, some embedded in the side of the hull, suggest that it was attacked, perhaps by pirates. It may be that the crew were taken prisoner to be sold as slaves, and the ship robbed of any valuable cargo before being sunk to destroy the evidence.

Today the Kyrenia Ship is preserved in polythene glycol (PEG) and is on display in the Kyrenia Crusader Castle.

*A model of the Kyrenia Ship, housed in the Manchester Museum, UK. Between 1982 and 1985, the* Kyrenia II *was built near Athens and was launched on 22 August. In April 1986, this ship repeated Kyrenia's final voyage, averaging just over 2 knots.*

## CARBON DATING

All living things absorb carbon when they are alive, and after they die the amount of radioactivity in the carbon begins to decrease at a very uniform rate. Archaeologists can use a small sample of anything that once lived (wood, leather, bone etc.) to measure the level of radioactivity in the carbon and find out how old the object is. Carbon dating is accurate to within 50–100 years either way, making it a very important archaeological tool. It was used to test timbers and foodstuffs from the Kyrenia Ship, giving an approximate date of 389 BC.

# THE MYSTERY OF LINEAR B

When Sir Arthur Evans was excavating Knossos in 1900 he discovered some clay tablets with strange inscriptions on them. He was to collect about 2,000 of these altogether, and he tried to decipher the writing, which he called 'Linear B'. He thought it 'may well be some primitive sort of Greek', but got no further than that. Similar tablets were then found at the Mycenaean palace of Pylos in 1939, and at Mycenae in 1950.

Linear B remained a mystery until 1952 when a British architect named Michael Ventris finally cracked the code. He worked out that the script was an early form of Greek, and that the tablets were records of trade, listing goods, equipment and people (presumably slaves).

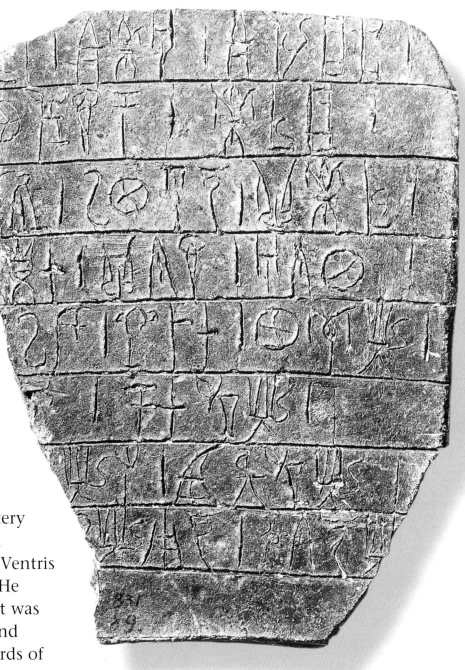

*A fragment of Linear B script from Mycenae. These tablets often list information about numbers of sheep, rams, goats and pigs.*

# MICHAEL VENTRIS

Michael Ventris (1922–1956) showed an early interest in Linear B when, as an 18-year-old, he daringly published an article in America about the Minoan language. In 1951 the Linear B tablets found at Pylos were published, and this gave Ventris plenty of examples to work on. In July 1952 he announced his theory that Linear B was an ancient form of Greek dating from about 1400 BC.

Understanding Linear B was an important discovery because the tablets provided a huge amount of information about the ancient Greek world. For example, until the code was cracked by Ventris, archaeologists had no idea that flax (linen) was grown around Pylos or that it was important to the ancient Greeks. The tablets show that there was a large textile industry based on flax, which was traded around the Peloponnese. This area continued to produce flax right up to the twentieth century.

*A black-figure vase dating from the sixth century BC, showing cloth merchants at work, carefully weighing the bales of cloth.*

# POTTERY

Archaeologists have found huge amounts of pottery at sites all over Greece. Sometimes many shards from the same pot are found together and the pot can be reconstructed.

Reconstructions have revealed that ancient Greek pottery was often very well made and beautifully painted. The two most popular types of pottery are known as 'black figure' (where a red pot was decorated with black figures) and 'red figure' (where a black pot was decorated with red figures). The detailed paintings on pottery have provided archaeologists with valuable information about religion, warfare and everyday life in ancient Greece.

*When pottery is excavated, it is necessary to wash it carefully before examination. Each piece is marked with the date and the position where it was found.*

Pottery is useful to archaeologists in other ways too. By looking closely at the clay a pot was made from, they can work out where it was made. If a pot was found a long way from its place of manufacture – in southern Russia, for example – ancient Greek trade routes can be worked out.

By studying the way pots were made and their many different styles, a dating sequence can be established. This sequence becomes even more reliable when examples of pottery are found at a site that has a known date. For example, burnt pottery found in Athens at the correct layer may 'connect' with the Persian destruction of the city in 480 BC. If so, the pottery can be correctly 'slotted' into the dating sequence.

*A dinos or wine-mixing bowl on a stand, made by Sophilos, one of the first well-known ancient Greek vase painters.*

# THERMOLUMINESCENCE

Pottery is made from clay, and the minerals found in clay store energy from any nuclear radiation it is exposed to. If clay is heated to above 500 degrees centigrade (such as when a pot is fired to harden it) the stored energy is given off as light. This light is called thermoluminescence. When the heating is finished the clay pot will begin to store energy again. Archaeologists use special scientific equipment to work out when a pot was last heated, and hence when it was made.

# PRESERVING THE PAST

Discovering sites and excavating artefacts from the ground is only part of an archaeologist's work. Sites and artefacts must be cared for and conserved for the future.

A serious problem facing the ancient monuments of Greece is the pressure of the modern world. The Acropolis is in grave danger from air pollution which is damaging the surfaces of the marble monuments, and from tourism. The millions of tourists who visit every year are actually wearing away the rock with their feet! Traffic vibrations are also causing damage to the monuments.

*The temple of Athena Nike on the Acropolis undergoing important restoration work. Note the huge number of tourists climbing up the rock.*

Because of this, all of the remaining statues have been taken into the Acropolis Museum, and parts of the standing monuments have been protected by wooden roofs. Measures to try and reduce air pollution in Athens have been introduced, and cars are no longer allowed to drive up to the base of the Acropolis, in an effort to try and reduce vibration. Sadly, tourists are no longer allowed inside the monuments as they once were.

Long-term restoration work is currently taking place at the Erectheion on the Acropolis. This impressive temple was built at the end of the fifth century BC to house a statue of Athena. The famous Porch of the Carytids – statues of women holding up the roof – and the beautiful marble walls were in a terrible condition by the late 1970s. Something had to be done to arrest and repair the damage. Lord Elgin had taken one of the Carytids back to London, so part of the restoration process involved filling the empty space with a replica statue.

*The beautiful marble Carytid in splendid isolation in the British Museum, taken from her home in the Erectheion by Lord Elgin.*

# WHAT NEXT?

Today, archaeologists working in Greece and her ancient colonies tend to combine different approaches. A site may require the painstaking work of field walking and surveying in one area, some small-scale excavation in another, and a major dig in yet another. Sometimes archaeologists deliberately leave a portion of a site unexcavated so that more advanced and as-yet uninvented techniques can be used to uncover its mysteries.

*Archaeologists carefully scraping and brushing the surfaces of their trenches. A lot of their work is slow and methodical, especially with fragile objects.*

Modern technology is changing the way sites can be understood. A combination of field walking to turn up surface artefacts and the use of ground penetration radar over a site can produce computer maps of what lies beneath the ground with no need for excavation at all. This method has allowed archaeologists successfully to discover ancient roads, bridges, pottery kilns, wells, graves, wine presses, farmhouses and even whole sanctuaries. However, sometimes excavation is still essential, as in 'rescue archaeology', where a site is threatened by the building of a new road, an office block or even a car park!

For the people of Greece the issue of the Elgin Marbles, presently held at the British Museum in London, remains unresolved. Many people, both in Greece and the UK feel that the Marbles should be returned home to Greece. The Greek government has been requesting this for years, but not until recently did popular opinion begin to agree with them. It may be that in the not too distant future the Marbles will be returned to the land where they were first made.

*The Duveen Gallery in the British Museum which houses the Elgin Marbles. Millions of visitors come here each year from all over the world.*

# TIMELINES

## ANCIENT GREEK TIMELINE (ALL DATES ARE BC)

| c.2600–1450 | c.1626 | c.1580–1400 | c.1450 | c.1375 |
|---|---|---|---|---|
| Minoan civilization develops. Knossos built (see page 6–7) | Thera erupts with terrible results for Crete (see page 7) | On the Greek mainland, the Mycenaean civilization flourishes (see page 8) | Mycenaeans conquer Crete (see page 7) | Palace at Knossos destroyed |

| c.776 | From 650 | 499–478 | c.448–432 | 431–404 |
|---|---|---|---|---|
| Olympic Games begin | Greek colonies started: the beginning of 'Classical Greece' (see page 10) | Wars between the Greeks and the Persians | Parthenon built (see pages 16) | Peloponnesian War: Athens v. Sparta |

## ARCHAEOLOGICAL TIMELINE (ALL DATES ARE AD)

| 1800–1805 | 1846 | 1866–1889 | 1870–1890 | 1882 | 1885 |
|---|---|---|---|---|---|
| Lord Elgin in Athens (see page 17) | French School of Archaeology at Athens founded | National Archaeological Museum built in Athens | Schliemann excavates Troy (see pages 8–9) | American School of Classical Studies set up in Athens | British Archaeological School set up |

| c.1250 | c.1125 |
|--------|--------|
| Possible date for the Trojan Wars (see page 8) | Mycenae invaded by northern tribes. Beginning of the dark ages (see page 10) |

| 338 | 336–323 | 30 |
|-----|---------|-----|
| Defeat of Greek city states by Philip II of Macedonia | Reign of Alexander the Great | Greece becomes part of Roman Empire |

| 1896 | 1900 | 1928–34 | 1931 | 1952 | 1977 |
|------|------|---------|------|------|------|
| First modern Olympic Games | Sir Arthur Evans begins excavating Knossos (see page 7) | American School excavates at Olynthus (see pages 20–21) | American School excavates the agora at Athens (see page 15) | Michael Ventris announces his theory about Linear B (see pages 36–37) | Discovery in Vergina of the tomb of Philip II of Macedonia (see page 31) |

# GLOSSARY

**acropolis** the highest and best defended part of a Greek city.

**agora** a group of important buildings around a market-place.

**artefacts** objects, such as tools or pots, that help archaeologists find out how people lived.

**Athena** Greek goddess of war and arts and crafts. Athens was named after her.

**cella** the most sacred part of a temple or shrine.

**city-state (*polis*)** a city, with its surrounding area that was self-governing.

**corrosion** the wearing away of metal and other materials by chemical attack, for example by air and water

**crop marks** marks that can be seen from the air in fields with crops, which show there may be remains beneath the soil.

**dark age** the period in ancient Greece after 1100 BC when much culture – such as writing – was lost.

**democracy** a political system that originated in Greece which means 'rule by the people'.

**hoplite** a Greek footsoldier armed with a spear and protected by a large shield.

**Minoan** the civilization on Crete c. 2600–1450 BC. Sir Arthur Evans named them 'Minoan' after the legendary King Minos.

**Mycenae** the city state of Mycenae which was at its peak c. 1400 BC.

**pediment** low triangular wall between the pitched roof and columns at the narrow ends of large Greek buildings such as temples.

**resistivity** a way of 'seeing into the ground' using electricity. Solid objects produce high resistance, while hollow areas produce low resistance.

**shadow marks** aerial photographs taken of the ground when the sun is low in the sky show up hollows and bumps which can betray the presence of buried features.

**shard** a broken piece of pottery or glass.

**soil marks** aerial photographs of ploughed fields can reveal different soil colours which may indicate the presence of a buried feature.

**spoil** the waste – soil and stones – from an excavation. It is usually dumped into a spoil heap which is checked every evening for any artefacts that might have slipped through.

**treasuries** found in sanctuaries, these held the big votive offerings from the city states and individuals.

**trireme** a Greek warship, propelled by 170 oarsmen organized in three levels, hence the name.

**votive offering** an offering to the gods, in the hope of a blessing or a favour in return.

# FURTHER INFORMATION

## PLACES TO VISIT

**Britain**
Ashmolean Museum of Art
and Archaeology,
Beaumont Street,
Oxford OX1 2PH
Tel: (01865) 278000

The British Museum,
Great Russell Street,
London WC1B 3DG

**Crete**
Archaeological Museum,
Iraklion, Nr. Knossos
Tel: (+30) 28 10 226092

**Greece**
National Archaeological
Museum,
Patission 44 St,
Athens 10682
Tel: (+30) 210 8217717

## BOOKS

*Ancient Greece*
by Robert Nicholson
(Two-Can Publishing 1992)

*Archaeology*
(Eyewitness Guide)
by Jane McIntosh
(Dorling Kindersley 1994)

*In the Daily Life of the Ancient Greeks*
(Gods and Goddesses series)
by Fiona MacDonald
(Hodder Wayland, 2002)

*You Wouldn't Want To Be: A Slave in Ancient Greece*
by Fiona MacDonald
(Hodder Wayland, 2001)

*The Greek News*
by Philip Steele
and Anton Powell
(Walker Books 1996)

## VIDEOS

*From Knossos to Athens*
(Viewtech)

*The Elgin Marbles* (Viewtech)

## CLUBS

The Young Archaeologist's Club,
Bowes Morrell House,
111 Walmgate,
York, YO1 9WA

---

**Use this book for teaching literacy**

This book can help you in the literacy hour in the following ways:

 Children can read and evaluate the projects in this book for their purpose, organization and clarity. (Year 5, Term 1: Non-fiction reading comprehension)

 They can use this book to collect, define and spell technical words used by archaeologists or historians. (Year 5, Term 2: Vocabulary extension)

 The book is an example of an explanatory text in which children can investigate and note features of impersonal style. (Year 5, Term 2: Non-fiction reading comprehension)

 The discussion contained in chapters 12 and 13 can be used by children to draft and write letters of their own arguing the case for preserving the past for future generations. (Year 5, Term 3: Non-fiction writing composition)

# INDEX